Linux

A Complete Guide to Learn Linux
Commands, Linux Operating System and
Shell Scripting Step-by-Step

Written By Nicholas Ayden

Legal & Disclaimer

The information contained in this book and its contents is not designed to replace or take the place of any form of medical or professional advice; and is not meant to replace the need for independent medical, financial, legal or other professional advice or services, as may be required. The content and information in this book has been provided for educational and entertainment purposes only.

The content and information contained in this book has been compiled from sources deemed reliable, and it is accurate to the best of the Author's knowledge, information and belief.

However, the Author cannot guarantee its accuracy and validity and cannot be held liable for any errors and/or omissions. Further, changes are periodically made to this book as and when needed. Where appropriate and/or necessary, you must consult a professional (including but not limited to your doctor, attorney, financial advisor or such other professional advisor) before using any of the suggested remedies, techniques, or information in this book.

Upon using the contents and information contained in this book, you agree to hold harmless the Author from and against any damages, costs, and expenses, including any legal fees potentially resulting from the application of any of the information provided by this book. This disclaimer applies to any loss, damages or injury caused by the use and application, whether directly or indirectly, of any advice or information presented, whether for breach of contract, tort, negligence, personal injury, criminal intent, or under any other cause of action.

You agree to accept all risks of using the information presented inside this book.

You agree that by continuing to read this book, where appropriate and/or necessary, you shall consult a professional (including but not limited to your doctor, attorney, or financial advisor or such other advisor as needed) before using any of the suggested remedies, techniques, or information in this book.

Table of Contents

Preface

This book is one of the main books on the programming language. The main purpose of each of these programming books is to find better ways to teach/learn to solve problems using a computer programming language as a tool.

This book aims to serve as a fundamental tool in the teaching/learning process of a programming base, using a novel approach from the pedagogical point of view and modern from the technological point of view.

We want the book to be a work tool within a learning process, in which the reader must be its main protagonist. For this reason, along with the levels that make up the book, it may be that the reader will be asked to perform small exercises as the theory is presented and then to solve complete problems directly on the book using language main of the book that is Linux.

The book is aimed at students who take a computer programming course for the first time, regardless of the study program, they are following. This means that to use the book, no specific previous training is needed and that the competencies generated with this text can be easily framed within any professional profile.

Who Should Read This Book?

Did you know that:

Does Linux already have almost 30 years of history?

This system is essential for any computer programmer or administrator?

Linux is the free software is widespread in the world?

Linux has evolved in these years not only thanks to Torvalds but also thanks to anonymous people who contribute to the improvement of this system by vocation.

It was an accident. Or so says Linus Torvalds, the creator of Linux. Almost 30 years ago, this Finn began to program what we know today as the Linux system. Today, that accident has become the most used free software in the world and one of the essentials for all computer scientists.

So you can already get an idea of how important it can be to know Linux in-depth to dedicate yourself to computing today. Not everything depends on big companies like Microsoft. The adaptability of this software with a simple change introduced in its programming makes it perfect for any purpose, precisely, for this reason, it is present worldwide.

The importance of Linux in the world of computing far from descending is destined to rise. Linux is the system used in large calculation centers, so large companies are increasingly demanding professionals to handle it; from computers, through industrial systems, servers and even mobile phones.

Almost 85% of servers distributed on the Internet are running Linux. Be aware or not, you are using Linux directly or indirectly in your daily life. Are you a Google user to search the Internet? Do you buy books on Amazon? Do you invest in shares on the New York Stock Exchange? Well, the infrastructure of these companies depends entirely on this operating system.

There is no doubt that this book is for you because Linux is for information technology professionals (programmers, developers, telematics, security professionals, network professionals, etc.). Linux represents a world of knowledge and possibilities since it offers all kinds of tools and technologies totally free. Within the world of Linux and Free, Software knowledge circulates freely without restrictions through the Internet.

We encourage you to learn Linux today. So you can update your professional profile and achieve all your goals in a short time.

How to Read This Book?

This is a codebook. These types of books are the simplest books and it is very common to see them at the tables of beginners and some engineers. They are the friendliest books in the sense that they contain many examples that can be copied directly to the computer to see them work and the explanations are not too difficult to understand.

So, it is virtually possible to place the book next to the screen and type the codes while reading the explanations.

To read this book, it is prudent to first read all the parts written with words and descriptions without worrying too much about understanding the examples. If anything, you can try to compile some of the simplest examples just to get an idea about what one is reading. In the first reading, it is important to calmly read all the descriptions. And in the case of appendices that include compendiums of calls to functions and libraries, it is enough to know that there are such functions and what they are capable of doing, regardless of whether you do not understand how they work. Once you finish reading all these parts calmly, when you put the book next to the PC, go into bullet-time and start typing and compiling all the examples.

As you type, all the things you have read will come to your mind and it will be much easier to locate and repair the errors or at least you will have an idea on which pages to look for the answers. Once you have just typed in the codes and played with them by changing things you can consider that you will get what you need from this document.

Good luck!

Introduction

As an operating system, Linux is very efficient and has an excellent design. It is multitasking, multi-user, multiplatform and multiprocessor; on Intel platforms run in protected mode. It protects the memory so that a program cannot bring down the rest of the system. It loads only the parts of a program that are used and shares memory between programs increasing speed and decreasing memory usage. It uses a virtual memory system per page and all free memory for cache. It allows you to use linked libraries both statically and dynamically. It is distributed with source code; uses up to 64 virtual consoles. It has an advanced file system but you can use those of the other systems and supports networks in both TCP/IP and other protocols.

It was created by Linus Torvalds in 1991, at the University of Helsinki, in Finland, unlike Windows and other proprietary operating systems, it has been developed by thousands of computer users around the world, contributing all to get a Reliable, robust, powerful, reliable, secure and interactive operating system.

This operating system intends to bring freedom to users, to free them from the interests of the commercial sector and to bring, consequently, functional, robust software that meets the needs of users. This is not based on being one more product of the competition.

The meaning of GNU/Linux is that one, we already know Linux, the other, GNU is the name of the project that created the GPL license. GNU means "GNU is Not Unix," which is a very ingenious acronym.

In 1991, Linus Benedict Torvalds, a student at the University of Helsinki, released version 0.02 of its Linux operating system. Millions of users worldwide have this free system and many of them contribute to its continuous development, providing programs, information, etc...

In this eBook, we will go deeper into Linux and its open-source. This book contains 9 chapters with which, we will try with codes, solve problems, give information and all kinds of useful things to those who embark on Linux programming.

So, please read all the information that we are going to put into this material. Spend a little of your time and you will not regret it.

Enjoy it!!!

Chapter 1: Install virtual machines

In this chapter, we will see what is a virtual machine? What is a virtual machine used for and how to install a Virtual Machine on Linux (Ubuntu 14.04 LTS) to run Windows? To install a Virtual Machine on Linux we will use VirtualBox, which personally seems quite simple and intuitive to use. There are many other pretty good virtualization applications, such as VMware, Parallels, OPENVZ, ... but you can try them yourself if you want an alternative to VirtualBox.

In general terms, a virtual machine is any software that allows you to emulate the operation of a computer inside another computer thanks to an encapsulation process that isolates both. Something similar to the concept of Russian matryoshka dolls, which allow one doll to be inserted into another, but each maintaining the independence of its host.

A virtual machine is a software that creates an independent layer where the operation of a real computer is emulated with all the hardware components it needs to function (hard disk, RAM, network cards, graphics card, etc.) and that can run any operating system or program, just as a real computer would. All this emulation is encapsulated in a series of files that act as a container from which you run the virtual machine in a window of your computer as if it were a program and without anything that happens inside that window affect the computer running it.

Broadly speaking, the only difference between your real computer and a virtual machine that you run on that same computer, is that your computer does have real hardware, while the virtual machine emulates all its components so that it does not have to correspond with the physical hardware that you have installed on your real computer.

That way, you can adjust the hardware characteristics to make it compatible with the operating system you are going to use in that virtual machine. That is, even if your real hardware is not compatible with a certain operating system, that of a virtual machine that runs on that computer can be.

Once the virtual machine is created on a computer, you can copy or move the container file that is created and run it on any other computer, even if it has different hardware.

These types of virtual machines, known as system virtual machines, are best known by most users as they are ideal for virtualizing complete operating systems, but not the only type of virtual machines that exist. There are also process virtual machines, which are more common on servers and where only certain processes or services are virtualized and not the entire operating system.

What are virtual machines for?

There are several uses for virtual machines, but since they allow to emulate almost any standard operating system (Windows, GNU / Linux, macOS, Android, etc.), and since they run on a different and totally isolated software layer, one of the most frequent uses is to test different operating systems, programs or configurations with total security for your real computer since, if something fails in the virtual machine, this failure will not affect the computer that runs it at all.

That way, if, for example, you suspect that a file sent to you could be infected by a virus or malicious software, you can run it in a virtual machine to check its reliability. If nothing happens, you can use it on your computer. Otherwise, it will infect only the virtual machine and your computer will remain immune to the attack.

How to install a Virtual Machine on Linux (Ubuntu 14.04 LTS)

The first step is to download the ISO image from the Devuan ASCII installation DVD for the desired system architecture from the official download site. Select any mirror or use the torrent.

Open VirtualBox and create a new virtual machine of type "Debian (64-bit)":

Later, you must select the ISO image to use during installation. Select the recently downloaded image:

Then a virtual disk, preferably dynamically expandable, must be created to optimize the host disk usage of at least 16 GB and at least 512 MB of RAM (recommended 2 GB).

Before starting the virtual machine it is convenient (especially on a FreeBSD host) to configure the SATA disk to make use of the host input/output cache:

Start the virtual machine and select the graphical installation:

After selecting the language, location and keyboard, the system name and root password must be entered. Then the new user data must be specified.

Chapter 2: The Linux Directory Structure

Common directories

A directory is a set of files, which in turn can contain other directories. Directories also have permissions, and that is very important, to prevent inexperienced users from deleting or modifying something they should not. The directory tree helps us know where a file is located.

Unlike the MS-DOS/Windows systems, the UNIX systems do not divide the directories between the different physical units (C :, D :, etc.). On the contrary, for UNIX they are all files and directories. This will consider a hard drive or a disk drive as directories. Therefore, it does not make sense to write in the console "C:", but we will go to the directory associated with that partition.

All the files and directories of a UNIX system hang from the main directory called "root", which is represented as "/". The root directory is the basis for the entire directory tree, that's where all the directories in the system are contained.

When the user accesses a session, Linux "sends" the user to his working directory, which is his personal directory (/home/username). Where the user has the absolute freedom to do what he wants with his files and directories located there. However, you will not be able to do everything you want in another user's directory, since Linux has a permissions system that grants or restricts freedoms over directories and files in Linux. Although there is a "root" user, he does have permission to do anything on Linux.

Directory of most common Logs in Linux

- All logs are in the */var/log* directory in that directory. There are specific files for each application. For example, system logs, such as kernel activity, are shown in the *syslogLogs file*.

- In the apt directory you have a history.*log file* that saves all installation and removal records from the repositories.

- In the dist-upgrade directory it contains an apt.*log file* which stores all the information about the updates of the distributions.

- In the directory installer contains the log that is generated during the installation of the packages.

- In the *apport.log directory:* it contains files that are saved when the system fails.

- The *auth.log file:* includes information about authenticated logins when you log in via root.

- The *dpkg.log* file: stores in detail the installation of parcels and their disposal with the dpkg command.

- *boot.log:* Includes information every time the system boots.

- *kern.log:* saves information about the kernel as warnings, errors ...

- *alternatives.log:* saves information about installing and removing some packages when we use the update-alternatives command.

- Another important log is *Xorg.log* which includes information about the graphics drivers such as warnings, failures...

Linux File System Structure

The file system is a set of files that are organized in a tree, as seen in the following figure.

/

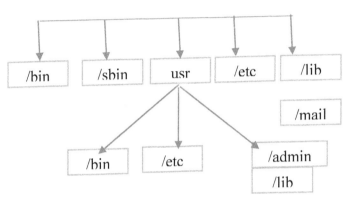

The Linux file system follows all Unix conventions, which means that it has a specific structure, compatible and homogeneous with the rest of Unix systems. The file system on any Unix system is not directly linked to the hardware structure, that is, it does not depend on whether a given computer has 1, 2 or 7 hard drives to create the c: \, d: \ or m:/ drives.

Comprehensive Directory Listing

The Linux file system follows all Unix conventions, which means that it has a specific structure, compatible and homogeneous with the rest of Unix systems. The file system on any Unix system is not directly linked to the hardware structure, that is, it does not depend on whether a particular computer has 1, 2 or 7 hard drives to create the drives c:\, d:\ or m:\.

As we said above, the entire Unix file system has a unique root or root origin represented by /. Under this directory are all the files that the operating system can access. These files are organized in different directories whose mission and name are standard for all Unix systems.

The Linux System has a very organized directory system, where each one has a function, these functions are defined below:

/root of the file system.

/bin Stores most of the essential programs in the system.

/boot Static files used by the system's boot loader.

/dev Contains special system files, known as device drivers, which are used to access system devices and resources, such as hard drives, modems, memory, etc.

- /dev/hda Primary disk

- /dev/hdb Slave disk of the previous one.

- /dev/mouse Used to read mouse input.

- /dev/hdc Primary disk in another slot.

- /dev/hdd Slave disk of the second slot.

- /dev/fdo They are usually floppy disk.

/etc. This directory is reserved for the configuration and boot files of the Linux system. No binary files (programs) should appear in this directory. Other sub-directories should appear under it:

- */etc/X11 X* Window configuration files.

- /etc/skel Basic configuration files that are copied to the user's directory when a new one is created.

- /etc/conf.modules File indicating which modules are attached to the kernel at boot time.

- /etc/fstab Install quotas.

- /etc/passwd Contains information about users, such as login, name and other information that the administrator wants to add.

- /etc/shadow Stores the password in encrypted form and their expiration dates.

- /etc/services Table in which the services to which users have access are described and by which ports they work.

- /etc/xinetd .d File to configure the daemons.

- /etc/rc.d/init.d Contains information to initialize the demons.

- /etc/hosts.deny Stores information to configure permissions on the services it offers.

- /etc/hosts.allow Also information to configure permissions on the services offered.

- /etc/sysconfig Stores system configuration files, for example language, keyboard type.

- /etc/inittab Contains the boot (boot) files of the system.

/ home: Contains the personal directories (houses) of the users. On a newly installed system, there will be no user in this directory.

/lib:These files contain code that many programs will share. Instead of each program containing its own copy of the shared routines, these are stored in this file. This makes the executable programs smaller and reduces the disk space used.

/mnt Mount point: Temporarily mount other file systems.

/opt: Additional applications

/proc: Contains special files that either receive or send information to the system kernel. Information associated with the kernel that is running, to obtain information on resources used in the system (CPU, memory, swap, devices ..) This directory is a virtual file system, that is, it does not physically exist on the hard disk, only in memory.

/root Home: (home) directory of the system administrator.

/sbin: Contains essential system programs, which are only accessible to the administrator (root).

/tmp: Temporary system files.

/usr: This is one of the most important directories of the system since it contains the data, programs and libraries commonly used for all users.

- /usr/bin: General purpose tools. There are also saved many of the Linux executable programs.

- /usr/doc: General system documentation.

- / usr /etc: General configuration files.

- /usr/games: Educational games and programs.

- /usr/include: Library headers of programming language C.

- /usr /info: GNU information files.

- / usr /lib: General libraries of the programs.

- /usr/local: It is designed for local customization of the system. Usually, much of the local software is installed in the subdirectories of this directory.

- /usr/man: Pages of the Linux manual.

- /usr/sbin: System administration programs.

- /usr/share: Data independent of the system architecture.

- /usr/share/dict: Word dictionary.

- /usr/share/doc: Varied documentation on the installed software.

- /usr/share/man: Manual pages.

- /usr/src Files stored by the source codes of different system programs.

- /var This directory contains temporary program information (which does not imply that its content can be deleted)

- /var/lib   Variable   configuration information.

- /var/lock Files for locks.

- /var/log: Contains miscellaneous log files. Most log files should be written in this directory or in appropriate subdirectories, such as the following:

- lastlog: the record of the last access of each user.

- message: system messages from syslogd.

- wtmp: registration of all accesses and exits.

- /var/spool: Spool area (track) of some applications. They are used to store data that is transitive, such as mail and news recently received or queued for transmission to another site.

- /var /spool/mail: Mail files of the different users.

Exercise: specify the top level directory when creating the zip file

Imagine that y you have a project with the usual directory structure (src/, bin/, ...), that is

```
project-name/

|-- bin

|-- lib

|-- src

`-- Makefile
```

And you would like to create a file with the following directory structure:

```
project-name-version/

|-- bin

|-- lib

|-- src

` -- Makefile
```

Is there a clear way to do this, to avoid creating a temporary directory? project-name / Elsewhere, then copying the files into a final zip -r ... call in that temporary directory?

(You are basically looking for some type of route prefix or relative route option).

Answer #1

You can use a symbolic link instead of copying everything

ln -s project-name project-name-version

then use *zip -r* via the sym link (zip dereference sym links by default)? When you finish you can simply *rm* The *sym* link.

Answer #2

This is more a tip than an answer: *use Git*!

If you set up a Git repository for your project, everything becomes quite simple:

```
git archive HEAD --prefix=project-name-version/ \

--format=zip -o project-name-version.zip
```

Deep Dive

In this part, we will see how to do a deep dive into Linux namespaces

Basically, we may refer to 7 types of namespaces which are Cgroup, IPC, Network, Mount, PID, User, UTS.

It is an abstraction layer that makes it appear that processes within a given user space have their own hardware resources isolated. Changes in global resources are visible to member processes of the same namespace, but not to processes deployed in different namespaces.

The main use of namespaces is the implementation of containers.

When you need to isolate a hardware resource to a process group (container), it will depend on the type of namespace. All processes are associated with a namespace and can only use the resources only associated with that namespace.

When you unshared you're caring

We can see the namespaces that a process belongs to! In typical Linux fashion, they're exposed as files under the directory /proc/$pid/ns for a given process with process *id $pid*:

```
$ ls -l /proc/$$/ns

total 0

lrwxrwxrwx 1 iffy iffy 0 May 18 12:53
cgroup -> cgroup:[4026531835]

lrwxrwxrwx 1 iffy iffy 0 May 18 12:53
ipc -> ipc:[4026531839]

lrwxrwxrwx 1 iffy iffy 0 May 18 12:53
mnt -> mnt:[4026531840]

lrwxrwxrwx 1 iffy iffy 0 May 18 12:53
net -> net:[4026531957]

lrwxrwxrwx 1 iffy iffy 0 May 18 12:53
pid -> pid:[4026531836]

lrwxrwxrwx 1 iffy iffy 0 May 18 12:53
```

```
user -> user:[4026531837]

lrwxrwxrwx 1 iffy iffy 0 May 18 12:53
uts -> uts:[4026531838]
```

Make the same attempt opening a second terminal. But this time again, run the same command. It's sure that you will find the same output. Do you know why?

Just because, as mentioned, the process has to belong to some namespace and unless you explicitly specify which ones, Linux always add it as a member to the default namespaces.

Let's meddle in this a bit. In the second terminal we can run something like:

```
$ hostname

iffy

$ sudo unshare -u bash
```

```
$ ls -l /proc/$$/ns

lrwxrwxrwx 1 root root 0 May 18 13:04
cgroup -> cgroup:[4026531835]

lrwxrwxrwx 1 root root 0 May 18 13:04
ipc -> ipc:[4026531839]

lrwxrwxrwx 1 root root 0 May 18 13:04
mnt -> mnt:[4026531840]

lrwxrwxrwx 1 root root 0 May 18 13:04
net -> net:[4026531957]

lrwxrwxrwx 1 root root 0 May 18 13:04
pid -> pid:[4026531836]

lrwxrwxrwx 1 root root 0 May 18 13:04
user -> user:[4026531837]

lrwxrwxrwx 1 root root 0 May 18 13:04
uts -> uts:[4026532474]

$ hostname

iffy
```

```
$ hostname coke

$ hostname

Coke
```

The unshare command runs a program (optionally) in a new namespace. The -u flag tells it to run bash in a new UTS namespace. Notice how our new bash process points to a different uts file while all others remain the same.

So, create new namespaces usually requires superuser access. From now on, you can assume that both unshare or your implementation are run with sudo.

Create and delete files and directories in Linux

We will begin by explaining how to create and delete files and directories. Whether to organize our personal content, or if we want to create a structure for a project, we will use the mkdir command for a directory called personal:

```
mkdir personal
```

If we wanted to create a complete structure of non-existent directories so far (for example: *personal/family/expenses/taxes/2016*), we will need the *-p* option of *mkdir*:

```
mkdir                                    -p
personal/family/expensives/taxes/2016
```

Create empty files

One may ask, what would be the purpose of creating empty files? The answer is simple. Empty files in Linux allow you to facilitate the practice of file manipulation tasks avoiding the delay of having to enter some type of content in them.

The following command will create an empty file called *file1* within the personal directory by using the touch command:

```
touch personal/file1
```

Insert content

To insert a text string into the previously created file, we use the echo command followed by that string and the redirection operator (>) that points to the file:

```
echo " I love learning Linux in CLA" >
personal/file1
```

(The previous option is also valid for the initial creation of a file containing the specified string).

To add (append in English) content to file1, we can also use echo, but this time you must use the append (>>) operator:

```
echo "The best training option in Linux and free software technologies" >> personal /file1
```

Create symbolic links

We can consider symbolic links as a reference to a particular file, similar to Windows shortcuts, but they have the following advantage in Linux. Suppose that to work, an X program has been compiled to use a certain file called Y. If the latter is subject to change, at some point we can find several versions of it present in our system, such as:

- Y-version1

- Y-version2

- and so on.

How do we ensure that our X program always uses the most up-to-date version of Y (Y-version2 in this example)? The answer is to create a symbolic link to Y-version2 called Y. In this way, when X "asks" Y, what you will actually get is Y-version2. When there is a new change of Y, we delete the previous symbolic link, and recreate it with the new reference. This makes it possible that before the changes of Y, the X program does not have to be compiled again to point to the new version.

In our example, this would be:

```
ln -s Y-version2 Y
```

As we can see, after ln -s (the command and the option to create the symbolic link) the target file should go, followed by the name of the symbolic link (include full paths if this operation is not being performed in the directory where both - file and link - will be placed).

Delete files, directories, and symbolic links

To delete, we use the *rm* command followed by the path to the file or symbolic link:

```
rm personal/file1
```

In the case of directories, it is necessary that they are empty to be able to delete them with *rmdir* (for that reason it is necessary to delete their content beforehand):

```
rmdir personal/family/expenses/taxes/2016
```

Chapter 3: All about the Shell

The shell or shell interpreter is a program that allows users to interact with the system, processing the orders indicated. Commands invoked from the shell can be classified as internal (they actually correspond to orders interpreted by the shell itself) and external (they correspond to executable files external to the shell). In addition to commands, shells offer other elements to improve their functionality, such as variables, functions or control structures. The set of internal commands and available elements, as well as their syntax, will depend on the specific shell used.

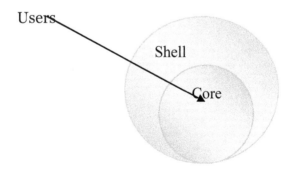

In addition to using the shell from the command line (based on the prompt as the indication of the shell to announce that it expects a user order), it can be used to interpret shell-scripts. A shell-script or "command script" is a text file that contains a set of commands and commands interpretable by the shell.

The shell is an executable file that must interpret the commands, transmit them to the system and yield the result. There are several shells. The most common is sh (called Bourne shell), bash (Bourne again shell), csh (C Shell), Tcsh (Tenex C shell), ksh (Korn shell) and zsh (Zero shell). Generally, their names match the name of the executable.

Each user has a default shell, which will be activated when a command prompt is opened. The default shell is specified in the configuration file */etc/passwd* in the last field of the line that corresponds to the user. It is possible to change shell during a session. For this, you only have to execute the corresponding executable file, for example:

```
/bin/bash
```

System indicator

The shell starts when reading its complete configuration (in a file in the / etc / directory) and then reading the user's own configuration (in a hidden file whose name begins with a period and is located in the user's basic directory, that is /home/user_name/.configuration_file). Then the following indicator appears:

```
team: /directory/current $
```

By default, for most shell, the indicator consists of the name of the computer, followed by a colon (:), the current directory and then a character indicating the type of user connected:

$ specifies a normal user;

specifies the administrator, called root.

The command line concept

A command line is a string of characters formed by a command that corresponds to an executable file of the system or, rather, a shell command as well as optional arguments (parameters):

```
ls -al /home/jf/
```

In the previous command, *ls* is the name of the command, -al and home/harrison / are arguments. The arguments that start with - are called options. Usually, for each command, there are a certain number of options that can be detailed when entering one of the following commands:

> *command --help command -? man command*

Redirects

Like any Unix system, Linux has mechanisms that allow redirecting standard input-output to files. Therefore, if the> character is used, the standard output of a command on the left can be redirected to a file on the right:

> *ls -al /home/jf/ > toto.txt echo "Toto" >*
> */etc/myconfigurationfile*

The following command is equivalent to a copy of the files:

> *cat toto> toto2*

The purpose of redirection> is to create a new file. In the event that a file already exists with the same name, it must be deleted. The following command simply creates an empty file:

```
>file
```

Using the double character >> allows you to add the standard output to the file, that is, it allows you to add the output after the file without deleting it.

Similarly, the <character indicates a redirection of the standard input. The following command sends the contents of the toto.txt file with the cat command, whose sole purpose is to display the content in the standard output (the example is not useful, but it is instructive):

```
cat<toto.txt
```

Finally, the use of the redirection << allows reading, in the standard input, until the chain located to the right is found. In the following example, the standard input is read until the word STOP is found. Then, the result is displayed:

```
cat<<STOP
```

Communication pipes

Pipes are specific communication mechanisms for all UNIX systems. A pipe, symbolized by a vertical bar (character |), allows you to assign the standard output of one command to the standard input of another, in the same way that a pipe allows communication between the standard input of a command and the standard output of other.

In the following example, the standard output of the *ls -al* command is sent to the sort program, which must extract the result in alphabetical order:

```
ls -al | sort
```

This allows connecting a certain amount of commands through successive pipes. In the following example, the command will show all files in the current directory select the lines that contain the zip element (using the grep command) and count the total number of lines:

```
ls -l | grep zip | wc -l
```

Shell-script in Linux

Invocation

In its most basic form, a shell-script can be a simple text file that contains one or more commands. To help identify the content from the file name, it is common for shell scripts to have the extension "*.sh*", so we will follow this criterion (but remember that it is merely informative and optional). For example, the following file would be a shell-script:

Script.sh

> *echo " Personal folder content:"*
>
> *ls ~/*

Exercises:

1. Verify that the "script.sh" file has general execution permissions (if not, it would be sufficient to execute "chmod + x script.sh").

2. Invoke the script to be interpreted, using for example the command:

cd ./script.sh

In addition to commands, shell-scripts may contain other elements, provided by the shell to improve the functionality of the scripts. In summary, the basic structure of a shell-script is as follows:

script_ejemplo.sh

```
                    <-- Shebang

                    <--   Comments (not
                    interpreted)

                    <-- Script Content
```

```
#!/bin/dash

# This is not
interpreted

echo Hello

ps w

echo " Process read
the script: $$"
```

As the content of the script, multiple elements (commands, variables, functions, control structures, comments ...) can be used, which will be analyzed in the following section.

The "*shebang*" allows you to specify the command interpreter with which you want the rest of the script to be interpreted when implicit invocation is used. The syntax of this line is the sequence #! followed by the executable of the desired shell, on which the following warnings should be made:

It is essential that it be the first line of the script, since, otherwise, it would be interpreted as a comment (starts with the # character).

There may be spaces between #! and the shell executable.

The shebang is not mandatory (when implicit invocation is used, if it is not indicated, an attempt will be made to use the same type of shell from which the script was invoked).

The use of the shebang is conditioned by the way the shell-script is invoked, there are 3 options:

Explicit: explicitly writing which shell you want to invoke and passing the script name as an argument, loading a new process for that shell (subshell or child shell process of the parent shell responsible for the command line from which the script was invoked). In this case the shebang is ignored.

Implicit: invoking the script as if it were an executable, which requires assigning execution permissions to the script. The shebang is read to determine which shell should be used to read the script, loading a child process (subshell) for that shell (if the script does not have shebang, for the subshell the same type of shell will be used as the one in charge of the command line from which the invocation was made). Note that shell-scripts are text files read by the command interpreter, that is, they are interpreted. They are NOT executed. The assignment of the

61

execution permission to a shell-script is a *file system* utility to accelerate the invocation of scripts, but whose internal function is to load a new shell process (subshell) so that it interprets the script.

Implicit with. (equivalent to import): the script will be interpreted by the same shell process responsible for the command line from which the script is being invoked. Consequently, in this case the shebang is also ignored.

In cases where subshells are created, unless otherwise forced (with `su -c` for example), the subshell will belong to the same user to which the parent shell that created it belonged. The user to whom the shell process that interprets a script belongs determines the operations that can be done from within the script (for example, if the shell belongs to the user `dit,` the script cannot modify the file `/etc/passwd`, while if the shell belongs to the `root` superuser, yes you can do it). Consider this aspect to determine what operations you can perform within a script, and with which user you should invoke it.

Exercices:

1. In a command console execute the command ps w and locate the process associated with the shell responsible for the command line from which you are working.

2. Invoke that script using the different invocation methods. For each of them, analyze the output obtained to determine in each case what is the shell process that is interpreting the script, the user to which that process belongs and if a subshell has been opened or not:

• Explicit:

/bin/sh script_example.sh

/bin/dash script_example.sh

/bin/bash script_example.sh

Implicit with ".":

. script_example.sh

Implicit: check that the script has execute permission and execute it with:

./script_example.sh

Modify the script by deleting the shebang, and rerun it. Analyze if there is any difference from the previous execution.

While both bash and dash follow the POSIX standard, especially bash adds multiple particular extensions, not supported by other shells such as dash. Consequently, every time we design a script we must take into account the shell or shells that support it, ensuring that it is invoked by one of them. To get an idea of the importance of this aspect, consider the following two scripts, based on the use of the structure for (to be used later):

script_estandar.sh

```
#!/bin/sh for VAR in 0 1 2 3

do

   echo $VAR

done
```

script_estandar.sh

```
#!/bin/bash

for ((VAR=0 ; VAR<4 ; VAR++ ))

do

   echo $VAR

done
```

Both scripts perform the same functionality, but *script_estandar.sh* is written under the POSIX syntax, while *script_bash.sh* uses a non-standard syntax supported by bash.

Exercises:

1. Invoke the script *script_standar.sh* (remember that you must have them already created in the scripts / directory) using the following commands, having to verify that they all work correctly and with the same result (the first and second calls really are the same, using the shell dash):

/bin/sh   script_estandar.sh

/bin/dash script_estandar.sh

/bin/bash script_estandar.sh

2. Now invoke the script script_bash.sh using the following commands:

/bin/dash script_bash.sh

/bin/bash script_bash.sh

You can see how, due to the non-standard script syntax, the second invocation works, but the first one (which uses dash) gives a syntax error.

General Shell Operation

The shell language is an interpreted language, in which lines of text (ending in \n) are read, analyzed and processed. The lines to be interpreted are read from:

- The standard input (default keyboard). In this case the shell is said to be an interactive shell.

- A shell-script file.

- The arguments, with the option when running the shell. Example: bash −c "ls − l"

With the lines read, the shell performs the following steps (in this order):

1. The lines are divided into different elements: words and operators. The elements are separated using spaces, tabs and operators. The # character is used to

include a comment, which is removed from the processing.

2. A distinction is made between simple commands, compound commands and function definitions.

3. Different expansions and substitutions are made. The command to be executed and the arguments to be passed are detected.

4. Inbound /outbound redirects are performed and items associated with redirects are removed from the argument list.

5. The executable element is executed, which could be a function, an internal shell command, an executable file or a shell-script, passing the arguments as positional parameters.

6. Optionally, wait for the command to finish and save the exit code.

When typing commands from the keyboard and trying to enter an element that is made up of more than one line. Once you type the first line and press Intro, the shell will display the secondary order request indicator > instead of the prompt, asking you to continue writing the item. When the interpreter concludes the introduction of the element, will interpret it, showing the command line prompt again. If you use the cursor ↑to try to see the command entered, you will generally see how the shell has rewritten the entry to apply the syntax with which the entire element is written on a single line. If you want to cancel the entry of a line (or lines) without deleting what is written, you can press Ctrl-C.

Quilting and escape character

The shell has a list of characters that it treats in a special way (operators) and a series of reserved words (words that have a special meaning for the Shell).

When we want to use a special character of the shell or a reserved word of the language without it being interpreted as such or to prevent an unwanted expansion or substitution, it is necessary to indicate it to the shell through the quotes (simple or doubles) or escape character, for example, to write the name of a file containing spaces, to pass the symbol <as an argument to a program.

The escape character \: indicates that the following character must preserve its literal value. The escape character is removed from the line once processed. If it appears at the end of a line, it means "continuation of line" and indicates that the command continues on the next line (it can be used to divide very long lines).

Quotation marks ": all text 'quoted' with single quotes will maintain its literal value, there will be no expansion or substitution and will be considered as a single word.

Double quotes ": it is equivalent to using single quotes, except in this case expansions and substitutions are made (all but the tilde and route expansions and the replacement of aliases that we will see later).

Quoting an empty string (" or ") generates an empty word (word that has no character).

Exercise:

Execute the following commands in the terminal and analyze the results:

```
cd

echo $PWD

echo \$PWD

echo '$PWD'

echo "$PWD"

echo hello \> a and b
```

```
echo hello > a and b    #the file a is created

ls

cat a

echo hello >"a and b"   # the file 'a and b' is
created

ls

cat a\ and\ b
```

Parameters and variables

As in any programming language, in the shell language you can create and use variables, which are called parameters here. There are several types of parameters:

1. If the name is a number, they are called positional parameters.

2. If the name is a special character they are called special parameters.

3. The rest are simply called variables.

Variables

The shell allows you to perform the following basic operations with the variables:

Definition only	VAR="" VAR=
Definition and / or Initialization / Modification	VAR=value
Expansion (Access to Value)	$VAR ${VAR}
Variable Elimination	unset VAR

On this, they should take the following observations regarding:

1. Definition and use:

- Variables only exist in the shell process in which they are defined (local to the process).

- Variables are only accessible from the moment of their definition down the script, that is, they must always be defined first and invoked later (a variable that is later cannot be modified). They can also receive within functions even if they have been declared outside them. In the POSIX standard all variables are global, although there are variants (such as bash) that allow the creation of local variables to the functions.

It is not necessary to define the variables prior to their use, since they are created by assigning them a value the first time. When defining a variable without initialization, its default value is the null string, that is, the following entries are equivalent:

VAR=

VAR=""

With the command set (without arguments) you can see all the variables (and functions) defined in the current shell.

2. Named

Keep in mind that Linux is "case sensitive" in general, which includes the variable name. So, VAR and var will be taken as two independent variables. For the name of a variable you can use:

- 1st character: a letter or underline character _.

- 2nd and subsequent characters: a letter, digit or underline character.

75

3. Initialization/Modification of the value of a variable:

- It is important not to include any space before or after the sign =. If done, the shell will try to interpret the name of the variable as a command (remember that the shell syntax is especially strict in terms of spaces).

- The value of a variable is always taken by the shell as a string of characters.

- If the value of a variable contains special characters, spaces, or other elements that can be misunderstood by the shell, it must be enclosed in quotation marks or it must include the escape character where necessary.

Expansion of a variable: the use of the keys {} is only necessary if just after the variable name you want to write more characters, without adding any space before. It will be seen later in more detail.

Exercise

Look at the content of the script script_variables.sh which must contain the following:

script_variables.sh

```
echo " Badly defined variable, order error
not found ":

VAR = 1

echo " Well-defined variables:"

VAR=1

VAR1=2

var=3

echo "Variables: $VAR $VAR1 $var"
```

```
echo "Variable VAR: $VAR"

echo "Variable VAR1: $VAR1"

echo "Variable VAR followed by 1 (requires
keys):${VAR}1"

echo " Double quotation marks: $VAR"

echo 'Single quotes: $VAR'

echo "Value: $VAR-1"
```

Check that you have the general execution permission. Call it and analyze its operation.

Chapter 4: Basic Commands and Directory Hierarchy

Display a hierarchy of directories from the command line

In this chapter, we will explain the use of the tree tool to list the contents of a directory in a tree type format.

On GNU / Linux and FreeBSD operating systems there is a tool similar to pstree, but to display directory hierarchies from the command line. For those who do not know pstree, this tool is used to visualize a process tree (according to the hierarchy defined by the parent / child relationship):

```
root@debian7:~# pstree

init──┬─acpid
```

```
├─atd

├─atop

├─beremote───4*[{beremote}]

├─cron

├─6*[getty]

├─ntpd

├─postgres───6*[postgres]

├─rpc.idmapd

├─rpc.statd

├─rpcbind

├─rsyslogd───3*[{rsyslogd}]


├─sshd───sshd───sshd───sudo───su
───bash───pstree

├─udevd───2*[udevd]
```

```
└─vmtoolsd────{vmtoolsd}
```

tree uses the same graphic representation, but to display directories.

To install tree on Debian and derivatives, run:

```
# apt-get install tree
```

To install tree on FreeBSD, run

```
# pkg install tree
```

By default, tree generates a tree with all files and subdirectories from a directory passed as a parameter (or the current directory, if none is specified), recursively:

```
root@abdul:~# tree /usr/local/share/ | head
-n 30

/usr/local/share/
```

```
    |-- applications

    |   |-- zenmap-root.desktop

    |   `-- zenmap.desktop

    |-- ca-certificates

    |-- man

    |   |-- de

    |   |   `-- man1

    |   |       `-- nmap.1

    |   |-- es

    |   |   `-- man1

    |   |       `-- nmap.1

    |   |-- fr

    |   |   `-- man1

    |   |       `-- nmap.1

    |   |-- hr
```

```
|   |   `-- man1

|   |       `-- nmap.1

|   |-- hu

|   |   `-- man1

|   |       `-- nmap.1

|   |-- it

|   |   `-- man1

|   |       `-- nmap.1

|   |-- ja

|   |   `-- man1

|   |       `-- nmap.1

|   |-- man1

|   |   |-- ncat.1

|   |   |-- ndiff.1
```

If you want to display only the directories, use the -d option:

```
root@abdul:~# tree -d /usr/local/share/ |
head -n 30

/usr/local/share/

|-- applications

|-- ca-certificates

|-- man

|   |-- de

|   |   `-- man1

|   |-- es

|   |   `-- man1

|   |-- fr

|   |   `-- man1

|   |-- hr
```

```
|   |   `-- man1

|   |-- hu

|   |   `-- man1

|   |-- it

|   |   `-- man1

|   |-- ja

|   |   `-- man1

|   |-- man1

|   |-- pl

|   |   `-- man1

|   |-- pt_BR

|   |   `-- man1

|   |-- pt_PT

|   |   `-- man1

|   |-- ro
```

```
  |  |   `-- man1

  |  |-- ru

  |  |   `-- man1

  |  |-- sk
```

It is also possible to limit the amount of levels to descend through the -L option:

```
root@abdul:~# tree -d -L 2 /usr/local/share/
| head -n 30

/usr/local/share/

|-- applications

|-- ca-certificates

|-- man

|  |-- de

|  |-- es

|  |-- fr
```

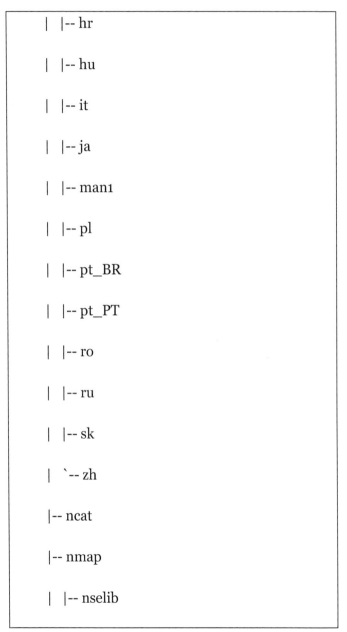

```
|   |-- hr
|   |-- hu
|   |-- it
|   |-- ja
|   |-- man1
|   |-- pl
|   |-- pt_BR
|   |-- pt_PT
|   |-- ro
|   |-- ru
|   |-- sk
|   `-- zh
|-- ncat
|-- nmap
|   |-- nselib
```

```
    |   `-- scripts

    |-- sgml

    |   |-- declaration

    |   |-- dtd

    |   |-- entities

    |   |-- misc

    |   `-- stylesheet

    |-- xml
```

If it is required to obtain the complete path of each file, use the option -f:

```
root@abdul:~#    tree    -f   -d   -L   2
/usr/local/share/ | head -n 30

/usr/local/share

|-- /usr/local/share/applications
```

```
|-- /usr/local/share/ca-certificates

|-- /usr/local/share/man

|   |-- /usr/local/share/man/de

|   |-- /usr/local/share/man/es

|   |-- /usr/local/share/man/fr

|   |-- /usr/local/share/man/hr

|   |-- /usr/local/share/man/hu

|   |-- /usr/local/share/man/it

|   |-- /usr/local/share/man/ja

|   |-- /usr/local/share/man/man1

|   |-- /usr/local/share/man/pl

|   |-- /usr/local/share/man/pt_BR

|   |-- /usr/local/share/man/pt_PT

|   |-- /usr/local/share/man/ro

|   |-- /usr/local/share/man/ru
```

```
|  |-- /usr/local/share/man/sk

|  `-- /usr/local/share/man/zh

|-- /usr/local/share/ncat

|-- /usr/local/share/nmap

|  |-- /usr/local/share/nmap/nselib

|  `-- /usr/local/share/nmap/scripts

|-- /usr/local/share/sgml

|  |-- /usr/local/share/sgml/declaration

|  |-- /usr/local/share/sgml/dtd

|  |-- /usr/local/share/sgml/entities

|  |-- /usr/local/share/sgml/misc

|  `-- /usr/local/share/sgml/stylesheet

|-- /usr/local/share/xml
```

Bash is a popular scripting tool available on Unix. It is the abbreviation of Bourne Again

Shell. It is a powerful tool for every Linux user or system administrator. Then let's start learning about Bash script in Linux!

Unix has 2 main categories of shells.

1-Bourne shell

2-C shell

Bourne shell is further classified as:

-Korn shell (ksh)

-Bourne shell (sh)

-POSIX shell (sh)

-Bourne Again shell (bash)

Bash scripts are a very powerful and useful component for development. You can reduce repetitive and short tasks to a single line. Many long commands can be consolidated into a single executable code.

Bash is available in almost all versions of Linux and does not require additional installation. The list of available shells can be verified by typing the following command:

cat/etc/shells

The result will be something similar to this:

/bin/bash
/bin/sh
/bin/tcsh

/bin/csh

Les scripts with Bash

To start with the basic command options, you can check the bash manual pages by typing:

man bash

Next, we will have to create a *.sh file*. For this we will use VIM Editor. To create a file, use a command like this:

vim sampleFunction.sh

Now we will be taken to the *.sh file*, where we can edit it.

This will generate a result with the Bash commands and their use. Every bash script in Linux should start with the following line:

```
#!/bin/bash
```

The following command shows the bash script path.

```
which bash
```

This will show the following result:

```
/bin/bash
```

The common syntax of bash is:

```
function functionName {
first command
second command
}
```

This can also be written as:

```
functionName (){
first command
second command
}
```

In a single line, this can be written like this:

```
functionName() { first command; second
command; }
```

```
caca
```

An example of this function is shown below, where we first create a directory and then change the path to point to the new directory:

```
sampleFunction () {
mkdir -p $1
cd $1
}
```

$1 represents the input argument of the command line. Bash can create dynamic entries within the command. To verify this function, you can execute:

sampleFunction myDir

Here myDir is a valid directory name. If you check the current working directory using the pwd command, you can see that you are currently inside the newly created myDir.

Likewise, any commonly used command can be added as a bash function.

Remember that when you have finished using the VIM editor to edit the *.sh file*, you can save and exit by pressing ESC to enter the command mode, and then type: wq to save and exit.

Basic functions of Bash

One of the basic examples of the bash function in Linux is shown below:

```
#!/bin/bash
testfunction(){
  echo "My first function"
}
testfunction
```

If you save this script in testFunction.sh and run it as *./testFunction.sh*, you will see the result as:

My first function

Echo prints the output on the console. If you exchange the position of the function definition with the call, this will generate an error. The following fragment will give an error.

```bash
#!/bin/bash
testfunction
testfunction(){
  echo "My first function"
}
```

Then, you will first have to define the function and then invoke it.

Bash functions can accept any number of parameters. The following example accepts two parameters:

```bash
#!/bin/bash
testfunction(){
```

```
  echo $1
  echo $2
}
testfunction "Hello" "World"
```

You can also use interactive tickets and perform bash functions. One of these examples is the one shown below:

```
#!/bin/bash
addition(){
  sum=$(($1+$2))
  return $sum
}
read -p "Enter a number: " int1
read -p "Enter a number: " int2
add $int1 $int2
echo "The result is : " $?
```

In the previous example, the value of addition is assigned in a variable sum, and this is what the function delivers. The interactive entry is taken using read for both numbers. Finally, the result is printed with $? which stores the $ sum value generated by the function.

Bash functions always return a single value.

You can leave comments inside the file by adding the # symbol to leave useful notes.

Bash scripts support:

Loop *while*

Loop *for*

Statement *if*

Logic element *and*

Logic element or

Statement *Else If*

Statement *Case*

Below is a brief example of the loop *While*.

#! /bin/bash

```
isvalid=true
count=1
while [ $isvalid ]
do
echo $count
if [ $count -eq 5 ];
then
break
fi
((count++))
done
```

The previous example uses the *while* and *if* statements. This executes the loop *while* 5 times before exiting after verifying the *if* conditional statement.

The result of this will be:

```
1
2
3
4
5
```

The *for* loop can be used to increase or decrease the counters. An example of the *for* loop is as shown below:

```bash
#!/bin/bash
for (( count=10; count>0; count-- ))
do
echo -n "$count "
done
```

The output of this loop will be:

10 9 8 7 6 5 4 3 2 1

In Bash && represents the logical element AND, while || represents OR.

With the If statements, we can also define *Else if*. Let's see an example:

```bash
echo "Enter a valid number"
read n
if [ $n -eq 101 ];
then
echo "This is first number"
elif [ $n -eq 510 ];
```

```
then
echo " This is second number "
elif [ $n -eq 999 ];
then
echo " This is third number "
else
echo "No numbers over here"
fi
```

The same example above can also be written using the case statement as shown below:

```
#!/bin/bash
echo " Enter a valid number"
read n
case $n in
101)
Echo " This is the first number " ;;
510)
echo " This is the second number " ;;
999)
echo " This is the third number " ;;
*)
echo " No numbers over here " ;;
```

esac

In the statement *case;;* It represents a case break.

Cat

The cat command in Linux is one of the most useful you can learn. It derives its name from the word concatenate and allows you to create, merge or print files on the standard output screen or another file and much more.

It does not require you to install anything, since it comes preinstalled with the coreutils package on any Debian or Red Hat based system.

Cat command syntax

Before we begin to delve into the subject of the article, we must log in to the VPS using SSH and quickly verify the basic syntax. The command takes a filename as an argument along with options to specify particular operations.

cat [OPTION] [FILE]

To find all available options, simply type cat – help in the terminal.

Create a file with the cat command

Using the cat command you can create a file quickly and add text. To do that, use the ">" operator to redirect the text in the file.

cat > filename.txt

This is how the file is created and you can start filling it with text. To add several lines of text, simply press Enter at the end of each line. When you are done, press CTRL + D to exit the file.

To verify that the file in effect has been created by the previous command, simply use the following *ls* command in the terminal:

ls -l

View the contents of a file with the cat command

This is one of the most basic uses of the cat command. Without the need for any option, the command will read the contents of a file and display it in the console.

cat filename.txt

To avoid scrolling through very large files, you can add the option | *more*:

cat filename.txt|more

You can also display the contents of more than one file. For example, to display the content of all text files, use the following command in the terminal:

cat *.txt

Redirect content using the *cat* command

Instead of displaying the contents of a file in the console, you can redirect the output to another file using the> option. The command line would look like this:

cat source.txt>destination.txt

If the destination file does not exist, the command will create or overwrite an existing one with the same name.

To add the contents of the destination file, use the >> option together with the cat command:

cat source.txt >>destination.txt

Concatenate files with the cat command

This command also allows you to concatenate multiple files into one. In essence, it works exactly like the previous redirect function, but with multiple source files.

cat source1.txtsource2.txt>destination.txt

As before, the previous command will create the destination file if it does not exist, or overwrite an existing one with the same name.

Mark the end of the lines with the Cat command

The cat command can also mark the ends of the lines showing the $ character at the end of each line. To use this function, use the -E option together with the cat command:

cat -E filename.txt

Show line numbers with the cat command

With the cat command you can also display the contents of a file along with the line numbers at the beginning of each one. To use this function, use the -n option with the cat command:

cat -n filename.txt

Show unprintable characters with the Cat command

To display all unprintable characters, use the -v option along with the cat command as in the following example:

cat -v filename.txt

To show only tab characters, use -T:

cat -T filename.txt

Tab characters will be displayed as ^ I

Delete empty lines with the Cat command

To suppress repeated empty lines and save space on your screen, you can use the -s option. Note that this option will maintain an empty line by eliminating only repeated empty lines. The command would look like this:

cat -s filename.txt

Numbering of non-empty lines with the Cat command

To show non-empty lines with line numbers at the beginning of each, use the -b option. Remember that the -b option will override the -n option:

cat -b filename.txt

Show a file in reverse order with the Cat command

To view the contents of a file in reverse order, starting with the last line and ending with the first, simply use the tac command, which is cat inverted:

tac filename.txt

Standard input-output

Once a command is executed, a process is created. This process opens three flows:

stdin, called standard input, in which case the process reads the input data. By default, stdin refers to the keyboard. STDIN is identified with the number 0.

stdout, called standard output, in which case the process writes the output data. By default, stdout refers to the screen. STDOUT is identified with the number 1.

stderr, called standard error, in which case the process writes the error messages. By default, stderr refers to the screen. STDERR is identified with the number 2.

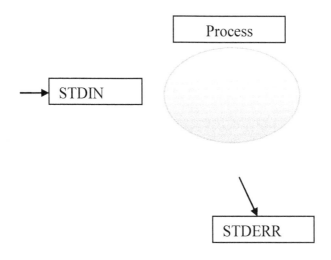

Therefore, by default, each time a program is run, the data is read from the keyboard and the program sends its output and its errors to the screen. However, it is also possible to read data from any input device, even from a file, and send the output to a display device, a file, etc.

Capter 5: Basic Linux Commands

Using the command line in Linux at first may seem scary, but the truth is that once you get used to them, then you miss them.

1-Help and Documentation: *man*

Man is one of the most useful commands you can find Linux.

It is a help command that shows information about the command and the various attributes that can be used.

To test it we just have to write in the terminal:]

 # man command

2-List Files and Folders: *ls*

The next command you should know is *ls*.

It serves to list the files and folders inside the directory you are in.

110

If by default you are in */home/* then it will show you everything inside.

To run it simply type:

 # ls/ path / of the / directory /

Or if you are already in that directory:

 # ls

3-AND-OR Lists

An AND list is a sequence of pipes (keep in mind that a pipe can be just a simple command) separated by the && operator. The format is:

pipe1 [&& pipe2...]

The pipes are running from left to right until one of them returns a non-zero value. No expansion is made in a pipe until the shell determines that it has to run that pipe (it will depend on the result of the previous pipe).

An OR list is a sequence of pipes separated by the operator ||. The format is:

pipe1 [|| pipe2...]

An AND-OR list is the result of combining AND and / or OR lists on the same line. The operators && and || they are evaluated with the same priority from left to right. Example:

pipe1 || pipe2 && pipe3

5-Change Directory: *cd*

The cd command is used to change directories, for example if you are *in / home / directory /* and you want to go *to / home / directory2 /*, you should type:

 # cd / home / directory2 /

If you would like to go to the top directory, read / home /, you can type:

 # cd ..

6-Lists

Lists are sequences of one or more AND-OR lists separated by operators; or &. Operators;

and & cannot appear in a row (for example, it would give error prog1 &; prog2)

Depending on the operator, the lists can be sequential, asynchronous or mixed (combination of both).

7-Sequential lists

The operator is used as a separator; The different commands are executed sequentially (a command is not executed until the previous one is finished). Each AND-OR list must be terminated by the operator; except for the last one where it is optional. The format is:

listAND-OR1 [; listAND-OR2 ...] [;]

8-Asynchronous lists

The & operator is used as a separator. The various commands are executed without waiting for the previous command to end (background execution). The format is:

listAND-OR1 & [listAND-OR2 &]

In this case, unless an explicit redirection of the standard input is made, if a background program reads from the standard input it will receive an end-of-file (EOF) error.

9-Mixed lists

They are combinations of sequential and asynchronous lists. For example:

```
lANDOR1 & lANDOR2 [ ; ]              #
asynchronous and sequential
```

```
lANDOR1 ; lANDOR2 &                  #
sequential and asynchronous
```

```
lANDOR1 & lANDOR2 & lANDOR3 ;
lANDOR4 # asynchronous and sequential
```

> lANDOR1 ; lANDOR2 & lANDOR3   #
> secuencial, asynchronous a, secuencial

10-Create a New Directory: *mkdir*

The mkdir command is used to create a new directory.

You have to take into account that you create it by default in the address where you are (it always indicates it in the terminal).

If you wanted to create it in another directory you should include the path, for example:

 # mkdir / newdirectory /

Or

 # mkdir/route/del/new directory /

11-Create a New File: *touch*

This command is used to create a new empty file if it does not exist.

For example if you want to create a new text file to leave a note, you can type:

 # touch file.txt

If you want to create it in another route:

 # touch /route/file/txt

12-Delete a File / Directory: *rm*

If you want to delete any file or directory you can use the rm command.

For this you will use:

 # rm achivo.txt

Or:

 # rm /route/file/txt

If you want to delete a directory that contains more files, you can use the *-r attribute*, that is:
116

 # rm -r / directory /

or

 # rm .r /route /from /directory /

13-Copy a File / Directory: *cp*

When copying files you need the cp command.

You have to find the source route and the destination route, in this order:

 # cp /routeorigen/file.txt /routedestination/file.txt

14-View the Contents of a File: *cat*

Cat serves to view the content of an asset without editing it. It simply shows us its content without the possibility of changing it.

 # cat file.txt

15-Edit a File: *vi/nano*

Vim and nano are two text editors.

Vim usually comes by default in all systems, although nano may have to install it. This varies from one distribution to another, although as a curiosity in Ubuntu we can do it with # apt-get install nano.

To run these editors you will have to use the commands

 # vi /route/file.txt

Or

 # nano /route/file.txt

Although nano shows the commands at the bottom of the screen (that's why it's so popular), vim doesn't show them, and so before editing it is recommended to type a #man

Better be cautious if you edit something important.

16-Switch to Superuser Mode: *su*

The su command changes to superuser mode or "root".

This mode is what you will need if you want to change something important or need permission to access certain files. This is the system administrator.

When changing to this mode it will ask us for a password, when you type it you will not see anything, so make sure you type it correctly.

 # su

17-Run in Superuser Mode: *sudo*

It serves to execute some order in superuser mode, also asks for the password before doing anything.

If you want to fire an order with administrator privileges you must type this command

 # sudo command

18-Change User Password: *passwd*

Change the password of the current user. Once again when changing it, check that you are writing it well (are the capital letters activated?).

 # passwd

19-Change Root Password: *sudo passwd*

Change the password of the root user, you do not need to explain the password again, right?

 # sudo passwd

20-Compress /Unzip Zip Files: *zip/unzip*

Compress or unzip a directory or a file in .zip format

 # zip -r file.zip filescompress

Or

 # unzip file.zip

21-Compress/Unzip Rar Files: *rar/unrar*

It works in a similar way, although with other attributes:

 # rar to -ro file.rar filescompress

 # unrar e -r file.rar

22-Restart System: *reboot*

Restart the operating system.

 # reboot

23-Turn off the System: *halt*

Turn off the operating system completely.

 # halt

24-Clean Terminal: *clear*

Clean the terminal text. It's always good to see what we are doing :)

 # clear

25-Leave the Terminal: *exit*

Log out of the terminal.

 # exit

Chapter 6: Teach Yourself Fish

Fish is a command line interpreter (such as bash and zsh), intelligent (in the sense that it feeds on the environment and user habits) and intuitive. Fish has powerful features such as syntax highlighting, automatic suggestions, completed by more efficient tabulation and having nothing to learn or anything to configure.

If you want to make your command line more productive, more useful and more fun without having to learn a lot of arcane syntax or configuration options, fish may be just what you're looking for!

Why do some people use fish instead of other command interpreters?

- **Automatic suggestions**: Fish suggests commands as you type them based on the history of previously used commands, just like a web browser.

- **Consistent scripts**: Fish is fully scriptable, and its syntax is simple, clear and consistent. You will never write esac again.

- **Completed from the pages of _man ***: Other interpreters allow automatic completion programming, but only fish generates that completion based on the content of the man pages installed in the system.

- **VGA colors**: fish natively supports term256, you will have 256 amazing colors available to use!

- **Configuration based on _web ***: You can configure the colors and see the functions, the variables and the entire usage history through your web browser.

- **Install and go**: You will be able to enjoy all the fish functionalities such as the one completed by tabulation, the suggestions based on the history and the instructions contained in the man pages, without learning anything new or anything to configure.

How to switch from Bash to Fish Shell on Linux

In the terminal, many users keep Bash. As a result, your terminal experience is not as good as it could be. It is very basic, without modern features out of the box. If you want a better terminal experience, consider switching from Bash to Fish Shell.

1-Install Fish Shell

Before moving from Bash to Fish Shell as your main terminal, you must install it on Linux. Fortunately, it is very popular and there are packages of it in almost all the Linux distributions that exist. Open a terminal and enter the following command to install it.

Ubuntu

sudo apt install fish

Debian

sudo apt-get install fish

Linux arch

sudo pacman -s fish

Fedora

sudo dnf install fish

OpenSUSE

sudo zypper install fish

Another way: its installation in archlinux

```
sudo pacman -S fish
```

After this you can try it without it being your default shell just run "fish" in the terminal.

If you want to convert it to your default shell (in archlinux) run:

125

```
chsh -s /usr/bin/fish
```

With this you should already run it without problems.

In case the above command does not work, it can be resolved by editing the *.bashrc file* and only by adding the following line.

```
fish &&
```

This will execute fish as soon as your shell is opened by default (Bash).

This can also be configured through your terminal emulator.

Fish has been around for a while, despite being quite modern in its characteristics. Due to its age, it is quite easy to obtain it in almost any Linux distribution. To install it, open a terminal and check your package manager to see "fish" or "fish shell". You can also check the official Github page and compile it from the source with the program code.

2-Change the punch to the fish shell

Using Fish as the main layer may take a while to get used to, as it is very different from Bash. Unlike many other alternatives (such as Zsh, Ksh, etc.), Fish is not using the Bash system as a base. Since Fish has this design, some commands may reject work due to a different syntax, and you may have to change some habits when using the terminal.

Luckily for you, there is a great page that describes all the complexities of Fish Shell and the environment to look at. Describe the syntax of Fish, how it handles the pipe and many other things. If you are considering making the change, do yourself a favor and give it a read.

Once you have reviewed the cheat sheet, it is safe to open a terminal and change your user's default shell from Bash to Fish Shell. In the terminal, run elchshmando. However, do not run it consudo, or you could potentially swap the Root user shell for Fish instead of yours.

++chsh -s / usr / bin / fish

Running the chsh command will assign its user the new shell. To get instant access to Fish with your user, type fish in the terminal Otherwise, restart your Linux PC to finalize the change. After rebooting, log in again and open a terminal again. If all goes well, Fish will be the new default and you will be received with Fish Shell, instead of Bash.

3-Configuring Fish

Although it has changed to Fish Shell, it is not completely ready to use. The next step is to configure it. In the terminal, create a new configuration folder.

mkdir-p ~/.config /fish

Next, create a new configuration file, within the new Fish configuration folder:

tap ~/.config /fish /config.fish

Using tap creates a blank Fish Shell configuration file with nothing in it. At this point, it is safe to add any custom settings in the shell. For most users, the only modification necessary is to permanently disable the welcome message. Add the modification to the Fish configuration by running the following command:

echo 'set fish_greeting "" >> ~ /.config /fish /config.fish

4-Fish configuration backup

The configuration of Fish on multiple computers can be quite annoying, since you will have to create a new configuration for each PC. A faster way is to create a backup copy of the file and restore it to each PC where you plan to use

Fish. To back up the configuration, run this command on the terminal.

cp ~/.config/fish/config.fish ~/Documents/

To restore the configuration, move the file to the new PC, place it in the Documents folder and run:

mkdir-p ~/.config /fish cp ~/Documents/config.fish ~ .config/fish /config.fish

For the most part, the fish is set up and ready to use. However, if you want to customize it and configure it more, there is a way to do it. Enter the terminal and execute this command:

fish config

Executing this command will automatically open a new tab in your web browser, with the possible aspects of Fish.

In the Fish_Config window, you can apply predefined shell themes, assign variables, configure custom functions, view command history, assign abbreviations, aliases and more.

Fish Autocomplete

By far, the most attractive feature in Fish is the autocomplete feature. It is far ahead of everything else, and this unique function is enough to convince even the most uncompromising Bash fans to see it. The best part of this function is that it does not require much knowledge to take advantage of. Even terminal noobs can get a great use of it.

To use Fish AutoComplete, go to the terminal and start typing a command. As you type, you will see that the shell tries to guess as it progresses. It is corrected as you receive more information. At any time you can automatically complete a command by pressing the right arrow key on the keyboard. After pressing the correct key, your final media command will be completed automatically.

Chapter 7: System Configuration the Structure of /etc...

Linux is a multi-user system, therefore, the task of adding, modifying, deleting and in general managing users becomes something not only routine, but important, as well as being a security element that is poorly managed or taken lightly, It can become a huge safety hole. In this chapter, you will learn everything you need to fully manage your users in GNU/Linux.

Types of users

Users on Unix/Linux are identified by a unique user number, User ID, UID. And they belong to a main user group, also identified by a unique group number, Group ID, GID. The user can belong to more groups besides the main one.

Although subject to some controversy, it is possible to identify three types of users in Linux:

Root user

- Also called superuser or administrator.

- Su UID (User ID) is 0 (zero).

- It is the only user account with privileges over the entire system.

- Full access to all files and directories regardless of owners and permissions.

- Controls the administration of user accounts.

- Performs system maintenance tasks.

- can stop the system.

- Install software on the system.

- can modify or reconfigure the kernel, controllers, etc.

Special users

- Examples: bin, daemon, adm, lp, sync, shutdown, mail, operator, squid, apache, etc.

- They are also called system accounts.

- They do not have all the privileges of the root user, but depending on the account they assume different root privileges.

- The above to protect the system from possible ways of violating security.

- They do not have passwords because they are accounts that are not designed to initiate sessions with them.

- They are also known as "no login" (nologin) accounts.

- They are created (usually) automatically at the time of installing Linux or the application.

- They are usually assigned a UID between 1 and 100 (defined in /etc/login.defs)

Normal users

- Used for individual users.

- Each user has a working directory, usually located in / home.

- Each user can customize their work environment.

- They have only full privileges in their work directory or HOME.

- For security, it is always better to work as a normal user instead of the root user, and when it is required to use only root commands, use the su command.

- In current Linux distros they are generally assigned a UID greater than 500.

/etc/passwd

Whatever the type of user, all accounts are defined in the configuration file 'passwd', located within the / etc directory. This file is of ASCII type text, it is created at the time of installation with the root user and special accounts, plus the normal user accounts that were indicated at the time of installation.

The */etc/passwd file* contains a line for each user, similar to the following:

root:x:0:0:root:/root:/bin/bash

abdul:x:501:500:Abdul
Harrison:/home/Abdul:/bin/bash

The information of each user is divided into 7 fields delimited each by ':' two points.

	/etc/passwd
	It is the name of the user, login identifier (login). It has to be

Field 1	unique.
Field2	The 'x' indicates the user's encrypted password, and also indicates that the / etc / shadow file is being used, if this file is not used, this field would look something like: *'ghy675gjuXCc12r5gt78uuu6R'.*
Field3	User identification number (UID). It has to be unique. 0 for root, usually the accounts or special users are numbered from 1 to 100 and those of normal user from 101 onwards, in the most recent distributions this numbering starts from 500.
Field 4	Group identification numbering (GID). The one that appears is the user's main group number, but it can belong to others, this is set in */etc/groups.*

Field 5	Comments or the user's full name.
Field 6	Work directory (Home) where the user is placed after login
Field 7	Shell that the user will use by default.

/etc/shadow

Previously (on Unix systems) encrypted passwords were stored in the same */etc/passwd*. The problem is that 'passwd' is a file that can be read by any user of the system, although it can only be modified by root. With any powerful computer today, a good password cracking and patience program is possible to "crack" weak passwords (so the convenience of periodically changing the root password and other important accounts). The 'shadow' file solves the problem since it can only be read by root. Consider 'shadow' as an extension of 'passwd' as it not only stores the encrypted password, but also has other password control fields.

The */etc/shadow* file contains a line for each user, similar to the following:

root:ghy675gjuXCc12r5gt78uuu6R:10568:0:9999 9:7:7:-1::

abdul:rfgf886DG778sDFFDRRu78asd:10568:0:- 1:9:-1:-1::

The information of each user is divided into 9 fields delimited each by ':' two points.

/etc/shadow	
Field 1	User account name.
Field 2	Password encrypted or encrypted, a '*' indicates a 'nologin' account.
Field	Days elapsed from 1 / Jan / 1970 until the

3	date the password was last changed.
Field 4	Number of days to elapse until the password can be changed again.
Field 5	Number of days after which the password must be changed. (-1 means never). From this data, the expiration date of the password is obtained.
Field 6	Number of days before the expiration of the password in which the user will be notified at the beginning of the session.
Field 7	Days after the expiration of the password being disabled, if it is not changed.
Field 8	Account expiration date. It is expressed in days since 1 / January / 1970 (epoch).
Field 9	Reserved

/etc/group

This file saves the relation of the groups to which the users of the system belong, contains a line for each user with three or four fields per user:

```
root: x: 0: root

ane: x: 501:

abdul: x: 502: sales, supervisors, production

cristian: x: 503: sales, Abdul
```

-Field 1 indicates the user.

-The 2 'x' field indicates the group password, which does not exist, if there would be an encrypted hash.

-Field 3 is the Group ID (GID) or group identification.

-Field 4 is optional and indicates the list of groups to which the user belongs

141

Currently, when you create the user with useradd, your main GID workgroup is automatically created, with the same name as the user. That is, if the user 'abdul' is added, the group 'abdul' is also created /etc/group. Even so, there are group management commands that will be explained later.

pwconv and pwunconv

The default behavior of all modern GNU/Linux distros is to enable extended protection of the /etc/shadow file, which (insists) effectively hides the encrypted 'hash' of the /etc/passwd password.

But if for some bizarre and strange compatibility situation it is required to have the passwords encrypted in the same /etc/passwd file the command would be used pwunconv:

```
#> more /etc/passwd
```

```
root:x:0:0:root:/root:/bin/bash

abdul:x:501:500:Abdul
Harrison:/home/abdul:/bin/bash

...
```

(La 'x' in field 2 it indicates that use is made of /etc/shadow)

```
#> more /etc/shadow

root:ghy675gjuXCc12r5gt78uuu6R:10568:0:
99999:7:7:-1::

abdul:rfgf886DG778sDFFDRRu78asd:10568
:0:-1:9:-1:-1::

#> pwunconv

#> more /etc/passwd

root:ghy675gjuXCc12r5gt78uuu6R:0:0:root:
/root:/bin/bash

abdul:rfgf886DG778sDFFDRRu78asd:501:5
00:Abdul Harrison:/home/abdul:/bin/bash
```

```
...

#> more /etc/shadow

/etc/shadow: No such file or directory

(When you run pwunconv, the shadow file is
deleted and the encrypted passwords 'passed'
to passwd)
```

At any time it is possible to reactivate shadow
protection:

```
#> pwconv

#> ls -l /etc/passwd /etc/shadow

-rw-r--r-- 1 root root 1106 2007-07-08
01:07 /etc/passwd

-r-------- 1 root root 699 2009-07-08 01:07
/etc/shadow
```

The shadow file is re-created, also note the restrictive permissions (400) that this file has, making it extremely difficult (that any user other than root read it.

/etc/login.defs

In the configuration file *etc/login.defs*, the variables that control the aspects of user creation and shadow fields used by default are defined. Some of the aspects that control these variables are:

1-Maximum number of days a password is valid PASS_MAX_DAYS

2-The minimum number of characters in the password PASS_MIN_LEN

3-Minimum value for normal users when useradd UID_MIN

4-The default Umask UMASK value

If the useradd command you must create the default home directory CREATE_HOME

Just read this file to know the rest of the variables that are self-descriptive and adjust them to your liking. Remember that they will be used mainly when creating or modifying users with the *useradd* and *usermod* commands that will be explained shortly.

Add users with *useradd*

useradd or *adduser* is the command that allows new users to be added to the system from the command line. The most common or important options are as follows:

-c adds a comment when creating the user, field 5 of */etc/passwd*

-d user's work or home directory, field 6 of */etc/passwd*

-e account expiration date, YYYY-MM-DD format, field 8 of */etc/shadow*

146

-g user's main group number (GID), field 4 of */etc/passwd*

-G other groups to which the user can belong, separated by commas.

-r creates a system or special account, its UID will be less than the one defined in */etc/login.defs* in the variable UID_MIN, in addition the home directory is not created.

-s default shell of the user when entering the system; if it is not specified, bash is the one that is established

-u user UID, if this option is not indicated, the next available number is automatically set from the last user created.

Now, there really is virtually no need to indicate any option since if we do the following:

```
#> useradd abdul
```

The user and his group will be created, as well as the corresponding entries in / *etc/passwd*, */etc/shadow* and */etc/group.* The home or work directory will also be created: */home/jack* and the configuration files that go into this directory and are detailed below.

Password expiration dates, etc. They are as wide as possible so there is no problem that the account expires, so practically the only thing that would be missing would be to add the user's password and some comment or account identification. How to add the password or password will be studied in a moment and seeing the options with '-c' it is possible to establish the comment, field 5 of */etc/passwd*:

```
#> useradd -c "Abdul A. Harrison" abdul
```

Always the name of the user is the last parameter of the command. So for example, if you want to get out of the default, you can set something like the following:

```
#> useradd -d /usr/abdul -s /bin/csh -u
800 -c "Abdul A. Harrision" abdul
```

With the above you are changing your home directory, your default shell will be csh and your UID will be 800 instead of the system taking the next available number.

Modify users with *usermod*

As the name implies, usermod allows you to modify or update an existing user or account. The most common or important options are as follows:

-c add or modify the comment, field 5 of */etc/passwd*

-d modifies the user's work or home directory, field 6 of */etc/passwd*

-e changes or sets the expiration date of the account, format YYYY-MM-DD, and field 8 of/etc/shadow

-g changes the user's main group number (GID), field 4 of /etc/passwd

-G establishes other groups to which the user can belong, separated by commas.

-l changes the login or user name, field 1 of /etc/passwd and /etc/shadow

-L blocks the user's account, not allowing him to enter the system. It does not delete or change anything of the user, it only disables it.

-s changes the user's default shell when entering the system.

-u changes the user's UID.

-U unlocks a previously locked account with the -L option.

If you wanted to change the username from 'abdul' to 'jack':

```
#> usermod -l jack Abdul
```

Almost certainly it will also change the name of the home directory or HOME in / home, but if not, then:

```
#> usermod -d /home/jack jack
```

Other changes or modifications to the same account:

```
#> usermod -c " area supervisor " -s /bin/ksh -g 505 jack
```

The above modifies the comment of the account, its default shell that will now be Korn shell and its main user group was set to GID 505 and all this was applied to the user 'jack' which as observed must be the last argument of the command .

The user 'jack' went on vacation and you make sure that nobody uses his account:

```
#> usermod -L jack
```

Remove users with userdel

As the name implies, userdel deletes an account from the system, userdel can be invoked in three ways:

```
#> userdel Abdul
```

Without options, it deletes the user account from */etc/passwd* and */etc/shadow*, but does not delete its working directory or files contained therein, this is the best option, since it deletes the account but not the information of the same.

```
#> userdel -r Abdul
```

Like the above, it completely eliminates the account, but with the -r option it also deletes the working directory and files and directories contained therein, as well as the mailbox, if the mail options were configured. The account cannot be deleted if the user is logged in or in the system when executing the command.

```
#> userdel -f Abdul
```

The -f option is the same as the -r option, it deletes everything from the user, account, directories and files of the user, but also does it regardless of whether the user is currently working on the system. It is a very radical option, in addition to that, it could cause instability in the system, so it should be used only in very extreme cases.

Change passwords with passwd

Creating the user with *useradd* is the first step, the second is to assign a password to that user. This is achieved with the *passwd* command that will allow you to enter the password and verify it:

```
#> passwd Abdul

Changing password for user proof.

New UNIX password:

Retype new UNIX password:

passwd: all authentication tokens updated successfully.

#>
```

The root user is the only one who can indicate the change or assignment of passwords of any user. Normal users can change their password at any time by simply invoking passwd without arguments, and can thus change the password as many times as required.

passwd has integrated validation of common, short, dictionary passwords, etc. so if for example you try as a normal user to change your password to 'qwerty' the system will show you the following:

```
$> passwd

Changing password for user proof.

New UNIX password:

BAD PASSWORD: it is based on a dictionary
word

Retype new UNIX password:

passwd: all authentication tokens updated
```

```
        successfully.

        $>
```

Note that when entering 'qwerty' as a password it was detected that it is a sequence already known as a password and it sends you the warning: "BAD PASSWORD: it is based on a dictionary word", however it allows you to continue, when entering the verification. That is, passwd warns of bad or weak passwords but allows you to set them if you really want.

Summing up then, you could say that is reduced to two command lines to create and leave a user ready to work on Linux:

```
    #> useradd ane

    #> passwd ane
```

The user 'ane' is created, useradd does all the work of setting the shell, home directory, copying initial account configuration files, etc. and then passwd set the password. It's that simple.

passwd has several options that allow you to block the account '-l', unlock it '-u', and several other options that control the validity of the password, that is, it is another way to set the account values in */etc/shadow* .

$> man passwd

Files Management

Normal and root users in their home directories have several files that begin with "." that is, they are hidden. They vary greatly depending on the distribution of Linux you have, but surely the following or similar ones will be found:

```
#> ls -la
```

```
drwx------ 2 ane  ane  4096 jul  9 09:54 .

drwxr-xr-x 7 root root 4096 jul  9 09:54 ..

-rw-r--r--  1  ane     ane        24  jul   9
09:54 .bash_logout

-rw-r--r--  1  ane     ane       191  jul   9
09:54 .bash_profile

-rw-r--r--  1  ane     ane       124  jul   9
09:54 .bashrc
```

.bash_profile here you can indicate aliases, variables, environment settings, etc. You want to start at the beginning of the session.

.bash_logout here you can indicate actions, programs, scripts, etc., that you want to execute when you leave the session.

.bashrc is the same as *.bash_profile*, it is executed at the beginning of the session, traditionally in this file the programs or scripts to be executed are indicated,

unlike *.bash_profile* that configures the environment.

The above applies to 100% text terminals.

If you want to configure start or exit files of the graphic session then, in this case, you must look in the graphic environment menu for a graphic program that allows you to manipulate which programs must be started when the session is started in graphic mode. In most distributions there is a program called "sessions", it is usually located within the preferences menu. In this program, it is possible to establish programs or scripts that start together with the graphic environment. it would be equivalent to manipulating 'bashrc'.

In addition, Linux allows the user to decide what type of Xwindow environment to use, be it a desktop environment such as KDE or Gnome or a window manager such as Xfce or Twm. Inside the user's Home, a hidden directory or file will be created ".", for example '*.gnome*' or

'.*kde*' where the custom user settings for that environment will come. Within this directory there are usually several directories and configuration files. These are extremely varied depending on the distribution and the environment. It is not advisable to manually modify (although it is perfectly possible) these files, it is much easier to modify via the graphic interfaces that allow you to change the background, screen saver, window styles, font sizes, etc.

Getty and login

agetty is the default getty in Arch Linux, as part of the util-linux package. Modify the TTY settings while waiting for a login so that the new lines are not translated into CR-LF.

You can usually access the consoles by pressing from Control + Alt + F1 to Control + Alt + F6.

- mingetty - A minimum getty that allows automatic logins

- fbgetty - A getty console like mingetty, which supports framebuffers.

- mgetty - A versatile program to handle all aspects of a modem under Unix.

How to add additional virtual consoles?

Open the file */etc/systemd/logind.conf* and set the NAutoVTs = 6 option to the number of virtual consoles you want at startup.

In case you want to start one temporarily, you can start a getty service on the desired TTY by typing:

```
$ systemctl start getty@ttyN.service
```

Virtual console: Login

The configuration is based on systemd input files to override the default parameters passed to agetty.

The configuration is different for virtual consoles and series. In most cases, you want to configure automatic login in a virtual console, whose device name is ttyN, where N is a number. The automatic login settings for serial consoles will be slightly different. The device names of the serial consoles appear as ttySN, where N is a number.

Edit the provided unit either manually by creating the following code snippet, or by running *systemctl edit getty @ tty1* and pasting its contents:

```
/etc/systemd/system/getty@tty1.service.d/
override.conf

[Service]

ExecStart=

ExecStart=-/usr/bin/agetty        --autologin
```

```
username --noclear %I $TERM
```

Serial console

Create the following file (and main directories):

```
/etc/systemd/system/serial-
getty@ttyS0.service.d/autologin.conf

[Service]

ExecStart=

ExecStart=-/usr/bin/agetty      --autologin
username -s %I 115200,38400,9600 vt102
```

Nspawn console

To configure automatic login for a systemd-nspawn container, cancel the console-getty service:

```
/etc/systemd/system/console-
getty.service.d/override.conf
```

```
[Service]

ExecStart=

ExecStart=-/sbin/agetty    --noclear    --
autologin  username  --keep-baud  console
115200,38400,9600 $TERM
```

Keep boot messages in tty1

By default, Arch has the getty @ tty1 service enabled. The service file is already passed --noclear, which prevents Agetty from clearing the screen. However systemd clears the screen before starting it. To disable this behavior, create /etc/systemd/system/getty@tty1.service.d/noclear.conf:

```
/etc/systemd/system/getty@tty1.service.d/
noclear.conf

[Service]
```

```
TTYVTDisallocate=no
```

This replaces only *TTYVTDisallocate* for agetty in TTY1, and leaves the global service /usr/lib/systemd/system/getty@.service untouched.

Setting time

Types of clock on the computer:

1. System clock: maintained by the kernel

2. Hardware clock: maintained by the bios

3. Date command: used to view and define the local system time.

-s, define the date in the format "YYYY-mm-dd hh: mm: ss"

Hwclock command: used to view and define the hardware clock.

--show -r, show clock information

-w, define the hardware clock as a system clock

-s, define the system clock as the hardware schedule

--set --date = "", to define the date and time of the hardware clock

Examples

Time zones: they form the standard that defines the specific schedules for each region of the world.

/etc/localtime, link to */usr/share/zoneinfo*

We will assume that we want any date, for example, January 18, 2013, 01:48 hrs, this will be done from the console with the following command:

```
# date --set "2013-01-18 01:48"
```

And ready, this will change the system time, now, to be more secure we will change the time of the bios so that everything is correct, we do this with the *hwclock* command:

```
# hwclock --set --date="2013-01-18 01:48"
```

And to prove that everything went well, type:

```
# hwclock
```

That will return something similar to:

```
Fri 18 Jan 2013 01:48:11 CST
```

Standard time

There are two time standards: localtime and Coordinated Universal Time (UTC). The local time ("localtime") standard depends on the current time zone, while UTC is the standard world time and is independent of the time zone values. Although conceptually different, UTC is also known as GMT (Greenwich Mean Time).

You can configure the standard hardware clock schedule through the command line. To check what time zone the Arch Linux installation has set, type:

```
$ timedatectl status | grep local
```

The hardware clock can be consulted and adjusted with the order *timedatectl*. To change the standard hardware clock schedule to use localtime:

```
# timedatectl set-local-rtc 1
```

And to configure it to use UTC:

```
# timedatectl set-local-rtc 0
```

Note that if the hardware clock is set to local mode, dealing with daylight saving time can be chaotic. If daylight saving time changes when the computer is turned off, the time will be wrong on the next boot.

Time zone

You can check the time zone that governs your computer with:

```
$ timedatectl status
```

You can list the available areas with:

```
$ timedatectl list-timezones
```

You can change the time zone with:

```
# timedatectl set-timezone <Zone>/<SubZone>
```

Here is an example:

```
# timedatectl set-timezone Canada/Eastern
```

This will create a symbolic link */etc/localtime* that points to a zone information file in */usr/share/zoneinfo /*. In case you decide to create the link manually, keep in mind that it must be a relative link, not absolute, as specified in archlinux.

Chapter8: Getting to Grips with Editors

In this chapter, we will see the 6 main text editors for the Linux desktop environment. Some text editors are not only a default editor for editing text, but also work as an IDE, which makes them quite useful. These are very useful in the development of the application in the Linux environment and although there are a lot of text editors out there, we will only focus on the top 7 text editors for the Linux desktop environment.

Commands to Create, Read or Edit Files

How to Create Text Files

We will use the most used commands when creating and reading text files from Bash. Let's start with the case of creating an empty text file, for which we will use the touch command.

1-Touch

The touch command will allow you, among other things, to create an empty text file (*in .txt format*) to which, later, you can add the content you want manually, or by using other commands that we will see.

```
touch filename
```

This option will generate an empty text file of filename, in the directory in which you are (by default the directory of the user with whom you are logged into the terminal).

```
touch filename1 filename2 filename3
```

In this case, the command will generate three empty text files, with the names filename1, filename2, and filename3, and in the working directory where you are.

Print the Content of a Text File

Following the case of viewing the contents of a file from the same console, the most useful commands in this regard are cat and more and less, each with its own particularities, as you will see below.

2-Cat

The cat command is one of the most used commands when it comes to handling text files (*in .txt format*) from the terminal. Among its many options, there is the possibility of creating a file, printing its content on the screen, etc. Let's see some examples:

This command will create an empty text file, named filename, and allow you to type the content you want to enter. Once the content has been typed, you can finish using the CTRL+D combination.

```
cat> filename

content line 1
```

```
content line 2

CTRL + D
```

This order will allow you to print on screen all the text lines of the text file of filename. The indicated file must be in the current working directory:

```
cat filename
```

This will print on the screen, together, the contents of the indicated files, in this case filename1 and filename2:

```
cat filename1 filename2
```

This command will print the contents of the text file named filename on the screen, also showing you the line number at the beginning of each line of text:

```
cat -n filename
```

Very similar to the previous one, with the difference that when numbering the file name lines, only those that contain text are numbered and blank lines are discarded:

```
cat -b filename
```

The *more* command is another useful command to print the contents of a text file on the screen. It is essentially the same as the cat command, with the difference that the more page command the content, and is more suitable when reading long files. Let's see some example:

This will allow you to print the contents of the file *'filename'* on the screen, but with the result paged. Thus, the lines that fit on a screen will first be displayed without scrolling. The rest will be accessible using the space key.

```
more filename
```

4-Less

The *less* command, like the cat and more commands, will allow you to read the contents of a text file. Unlike the other two, it will show you the content in text editor mode, and to move through the content you must use keyboard combinations.

With this option you can read the contents of the indicated file, moving through the different lines through the keyboard.

```
less filename
```

Once in text mode, you have several options to scroll vertically along the different lines.

One option is to scroll with the mouse, which if you use the terminal application that comes with the desktop environment you can do without problem.

If this does not work, you can use the keyboard scroll controls. Being in read mode, they should work without problem whether you are in the desktop environment or in a TTY terminal session.

Another option is to use the g key and then Enter. This will advance, by default, one line forward, but you can advance any number of lines you want, by entering the number just after dialing g.

```
.1
```

Another option is to use the space key. This will do something similar to an AvPag.

Finally, to exit reading mode and return to the terminal, you just have to press the q key.

Read and Edit Text Files

Finally, we end with *Nano* and *Vim*, two powerful console text editor, well known among the most geeks users. We will start with Nano, for being easier to use and learn, and we will end *Vim*, much more complex at the beginning. Both are text editors per console, but their common points say they end here.

5-Nano

Nano is a text editor for the terminal, which, rather than reading files, is used to modify and edit them, although for this guide we are also perfectly suited to open the file and view its contents from the command line. Here are the main options offered, so we encourage you to play with them to familiarize yourself.

First of all, let's see how to open the Nano text editor, something you can easily do with the following command.

```
nano
```

Once opened, if you look at the bottom, you will see that it shows the different combinations of keys that you will need when working with files.

```
CTRL+R
```

Combination of keys to indicate a text file to Nano to open it and display its contents through the console:

```
CTRL + V
```

Being inside Nano and with the file open in the console, this combination serves to advance to the next page.

```
CTRL + Y
```

Similar to the previous combination, this serves to go back to the previous page.

```
CTRL + W
```

This combination will help you enter a character or group of characters and search the text for any letter or word that matches the search parameter.

```
CTRL + X
```

To close the file once you have finished viewing it in the console. That will close the Nano text editor, and the Bash promp per console will reappear.

These are just some typical keyboard combinations, so you can move freely with Nano.

6-Vim

Vim is a very powerful console text editor and at the same time known among the most geeks users. Unlike Nano, which can be used with relative ease and ease from the start, with Vim the thing changes. Let's say the learning curve is much larger.

For starters, Vim does not usually come pre-installed in most distributions, but it should be available in the official repositories, so you can install it by command. In case you are in Ubuntu, Debian, or any derivative, you can do it with the following command:

```
sudo apt install vim
```

To open the Vim editor just open a terminal window, and type the following command.

```
vim
```

With this, you will see a small presentation text of the project. While there, you can open the Vim help file from the editor itself. Simply enter this small sentence, followed by Intro.

```
: help
```

7-Vi

The vi edition is a text editor that can be used in all types of terminal, its execution is full screen, it is able to handle the text of an entire file in memory and a few keys are enough to perform necessary operations.

Modes of vi

The operation of vi depends on three states or modes:

- The command or regular mode: it is the default mode of vi, where the keys allow actions to move the courses, travel the file, handle the text or simply exit the edition.

- The second, the insert or text mode: the keys enter characters in the text.

- And finally, last line mode or ex: where the keys are used to write commands at the bottom of the screen, on the last line.

vi survival guide

The syntax to run vi from your terminal is as follows:

```
vi'filename'
```

Once the file has been deployed you can scroll either with the arrow cursors or with the keys: h, j, k, l in case you don't have any cursor with arrows.

There are also other ways to invoke vi. For example:

If you only want to open the editing window are no files, use:

```
vi
```

In the case of common syntax, if the 'file name' does not exist, vi generates a file with the indicated name.

You can open vi with several files at once:

```
vi file1 file 2
```

Likewise, it allows us to open the file by positioning the cursor on a specific line, at the end of the file or according to the occurrence of a keyword. The examples respectively:

```
vi +45 file1

vi +$ file1

vi +/there was file1
```

Basic Commands

With a few basic commands, you can now work your file in vi.

Command	Description
: q	It is to exit the editor (without saving the information)
: q!	It is a forced way to exit the editor without saving the information (even if changes have already been made to the file)
: wq	Save the file and close the editor
: file name	Save the file with the specified name

Editing command

Command	Description

x	It is used to remove the character that is currently under the cursor
dd	It serves to delete the line that is currently under the cursor
dxd	It is used to remove x number of lines from the file, counting from which at that time it is under the cursor.
nx	It is used to delete n characters counting from the cursor at that time.
x >>	It is used for the idea of x lines to the right starting from the cursor.
x <<	It is used for the idea of x lines to the left starting from the cursor.

Search for and replace

To perform word searches, do it from the regular or command mode. It is as simple as entering the "/" symbol followed by the sequence of characters to be searched. Press the Enter key for confirmation. To navigate between the occurrences use the n key.

If what you need is to replace a particular sequence of characters, the syntax to use is as follows:

To do it in a line

```
: s / chain to replace / replacement chain /
```

To make the replacement throughout the document

The replacement can be made throughout the document with the following syntax:

```
%s/ chain to replace / replacement chain /
```

The best thing about this method is that it is extremely effective for searching through the use of regular expressions.

Copy and paste

The vi editor also gives us the ability to copy and paste a selection of lines. The process is simple, enter the following command:

```
nyy
```

Where, n represents the number of lines you want to copy.

For example, if the command you execute is this:

```
18yy
```

The result will be 18 lines copied to the clipboard. To paste the selection just enter the letter p.

Cut and paste

This process is similar to the previous one, but we replace the command with:

```
ndd
```

Similarly, n represents the number of lines to cut and finally to paste we use the p key.

Chapter 9: Environment Variables

Environment variables are a list of settings that save several states of a session. When a session is initiated either in the graphical environment or in a terminal, see the environment variables. In order to access the contents of a variable, you can use the echo command and the name of the preceding variable of a $:

```
~$ echo $LANG

es_ES.UTF-8
```

This command shows the language in which the messages will be displayed in the shell.

If you want to see the environment variables you are using, you have the env command. It will show you all the environment variables that are loaded in your session.

You can configure the environment variables by modifying the shell configuration files. In our case the default shell we use is bash, therefore the configuration file that we must use is: *$ HOME / .bashrc*.

```
~$ nano $HOME/.bashrc
```

One of the environment variables that can be configured is the PATH variable.

Where are the executables? $ PATH

When you enter the shell and execute a program, the shell must know where to find the executable corresponding to that command. This executable is a file with the same name that has written in the shell and that has the execution permission activated. For example, the cp command executable is:

```
~$ ls -l /bin/cp

-rwxr-xr-x 1 root root 109648 2010-09-21
```

```
20:32 /bin/cp
```

In this case the file */bin/cp* is an executable that belongs to the root user, but that everyone can read and execute and that is in the */bin* directory. Since the cp command is simply an executable file in bin to use it we should write its full path:

```
~$ /bin/cp fichero1.txt fichero2.bak
```

Although we could execute the command that way we have never done it. Somehow the shell has managed to find the cp command in the /bin directory even though we haven't told it.

When we try to execute a command, what the shell does is find the corresponding executable file in a list of directories that is stored in an environment variable called PATH. We can print this list using the echo command:

```
~$ echo $PATH

/usr/local/sbin:/usr/local/bin:/usr/sbin:/u
sr/bin:/sbin:/bin:/usr/games
```

In the example shown when writing a command in the shell, it will look for it first in the */usr/local/sbin* directory, then *in* */usr/local/bin* and so on until you find it in one of the $ PATH directories. If the command is not found, the shell will return an error::

```
~ $ hello

  The order "hello" was not found, perhaps
he meant:

  The "jello" order of the "giftshop" package
(universe)

  hello: order not found
```

When we try to execute programs created by ourselves or downloaded from somewhere we must take this detail into account. For example, if we download an executable called hello_world, and then try to execute it, the shell will not find it:

```
~ $ ls

  Hello World

~ $ hello_world

  The order "hello" was not found, perhaps
he meant:

  The "jello" order of the "giftshop" package
(universe)

  hello_world: order not found
```

The shell cannot find it because the working directory (".") is not included in the PATH. We could execute the command if we indicate to the shell the path in which the command is located:

```
~ $ / home / user / hello_world

  Hello World!
```

We could also use a relative path:

```
~ $ ./hello_world

  Hello World!
```

Or we can add the directory where the executable is located in the PATH. If, for example, we install a program in our home in the program directory, we can add this directory to the path and execute the program simply by running it with its name.

```
program:              /home/user/draw
circles/bin/draw_circle

we      add      to      the      path:
/home/user/drawjack/bin
```

```
new PATH: PATH = /home/user/cartoon
circles/bin: $ PATH
```

For the shell to load the environment variable, we can use the source command that will update the environment variables with the values that we have put in the file that we load, in this case *.bashrc*.

```
~$ source $HOME/.bashrc
```

It may be the case that we have the same program installed by two different methods. Both programs have an executable called the same. How can we know which of the executables is running? In Linux, we have the command *which* revolves the entire route. The shell goes through the path directories in order until one finds the executable. *which* returns the full path of the executable that the shell uses.

```
~$ which cp

/bin/cp
```

Home

Another widely used environment variable is the HOME variable. It refers to the personal user folder. For the user the folder is: /home/user

```
~$ echo $HOME

/home/user
```

We can change the value of an environment variable. The changes we make will only be seen in the terminal where we are. If we want the variable to "inherit" the applications we launch from that shell, we have to make the variable available, for this we can use the *export* command:

```
export PATH = /binaries: $ PATH
```

Therefore, in **the .bashrc** file we have to define the variables with export in front.

Exercises

1. Create a bin directory in your working directory. Use an environment variable in the command. Then add the directory to the path, for all sessions.

2. Create a new environment variable that shows your name. For example NAME. Make it can be used only in the terminal where you created it.

Conclusion

Throughout this eBook, we have seen that Linux is an operating system which has many benefits, such as free installation. It is also very efficient (load faster than Windows, for example) and contains many possibilities if we have programming skills.

On the other hand, that we install Linux on our computer does not mean that we should put aside the current operating system, being possible to combine Linux with other systems such as Microsoft or Macintosh.

Another point in favor of Linux is its security. It is very difficult for a virus or hacker to be able to attack a computer with Linux, even browsing without any antivirus this free software is much safer than almost any other with protection systems.

Other benefits we can mention:

- It is multi-user.

- It makes multitasking better.

- Efficiently supports virtual memory.

- In a network, it can act as a server (for example: ftp server or http server).

- It is very well documented.

We can conclude that Linux, rather than an operating system, is a powerful tool today, and that is why its use on Internet servers is increasing, and Linux is definitely very competent for Windows. For this same fact, large companies have adopted Linux, such as Apple Computer Co. that adopted the Linux kernel as the basis of their X operating system. Therefore, as we mentioned in the introduction, the knowledge you acquired through this eBook is not in vain. Just make a good application and you will see the benefits that it will bring to you.

Linux

CPSIA information can be obtained
at www.ICGtesting.com
Printed in the USA
BVHW041107160122
626379BV00015B/965